Polar Animals All Year Long

Melvin and Gilda Berger

SCHOLASTIC INC.
New York Toronto London Auckland Sydney
Mexico City New Delhi Hong Kong Buenos Aires

Photographs: Cover: Fritz Polking/Peter Arnold, Inc.; p. 1: Klein/Hubert/Peter Arnold, Inc.;
p. 3: Rosemary Calvert/Peter Arnold, Inc.; p. 4: Daniel J. Cox/Natural Exposures;
p. 5: Kim Heacox/Peter Arnold, Inc.; p. 6: Michio Hoshino/Minden Pictures;
p. 7: Chlaus Lotscher/Peter Arnold, Inc.; p. 8: Rinie Van Muers/Foto Natura/Minden Pictures;
p. 9: Hiroya Minakuchi/Minden Pictures; p. 10: Seitre/Peter Arnold, Inc.;
p. 11: Ralph Lee Hopkins/Photo Researchers, Inc.; p. 12: Daniel J. Cox/Natural Exposures;
p. 13: Roine Magnusson/Getty Images; p. 14: Daniel J. Cox/Natural Exposures;
p. 15: Tom Vezo/Peter Arnold, Inc.; p. 16: Thomas D. Mangelsen/Peter Arnold, Inc.

Photo Research: Dwayne Howard

ISBN 0-439-81534-7

12 11 10 9 8 7 6 5 4 3 2   6 7 8 9 10 11/0

Printed in the U.S.A.
First printing, January 2006

Few animals live at the North and South poles all year long.

Fun Fact

Most polar ice never melts—even in summer.

Summers are short and sunny.

Winters are long and dark.

Caribou live along the Arctic coast in summer.

Fun Fact

Caribou go from the coast to the forest and back every year.

They live in the forest in winter.

Whales find lots to eat in polar waters in summer.

Fun Fact

Whales usually give birth in winter.

Some whales swim to warmer waters in winter.

Terns fly from the Arctic
to the Antarctic in fall.

Fun Fact

Every year, Arctic terns travel farther than any other animal.

They fly back to the Arctic in spring.

Polar bears live in the
Arctic all year long.

Fun Fact

Lemmings grow long claws to dig in the snow in winter.

Lemmings do, too.

Many penguins live in the
Antarctic all year long.

Some seals do, too.

There's no place like home!